Science Inquiry

HOW ARE PLANTS POLLINATED?

by Emily Raij

T0050831

PEBBLE
a capstone imprint

Pebble Explore is published by Pebble, an imprint of Capstone.
1710 Roe Crest Drive
North Mankato, Minnesota 56003
www.capstonepub.com

Library of Congress Cataloging-in-Publication Data
Names: Raij, Emily, author.
Title: How are plants pollinated? / Emily Raij.
Description: North Mankato, Minnesota : Pebble, [2022] | Series: Science inquiry | Includes bibliographical references and index. | Audience: Ages 5-8 | Audience: Grades 2-3 | Summary: "Plants make pollen so more plants can grow. The pollen needs to get from plant to plant. How does this happen? Let's investigate pollination!"— Provided by publisher.
Identifiers: LCCN 2021002831 (print) | LCCN 2021002832 (ebook) | ISBN 9781977131393 (hardcover) | ISBN 9781977132567 (paperback) | ISBN 9781977154354 (pdf) | ISBN 9781977156020 (kindle edition)
Subjects: LCSH: Pollination—Juvenile literature. | Pollination by animals—Juvenile literature.
Classification: LCC QK926 .R35 2022 (print) | LCC QK926 (ebook) | DDC 571.8/642—dc23
LC record available at https://lccn.loc.gov/2021002831
LC ebook record available at https://lccn.loc.gov/20210028

Image Credits
Capstone Press/Juliette Peters, 7, 8, 9; Getty Images: JLGutierrez, 17, nechaev-kon, 21; Newscom/Hinrich Basemann/picture-alliance, 25; Shutterstock: Aliaksei Marozau, 13, d murk photographs, 1, 5, Designua, 19, Ellen Bronstayn, 14, geoBee, 20, Isabelle OHara, 27, Monkey Business Images, 4, 29, narikan, 28, Nikola Bilic, 26, Ondrej Prosicky, 22, 23, Peredniankina, 15, Phuong D. Nguyen, 24, RUKSUTAKARN studio, cover, ShoPrime Studio, 11

Artistic elements: Shutterstock/Tainar

Editorial Credits
Editor: Erika L. Shores; Designers: Dina Her and Juliette Peters; Media Researchers: Eric Gohl and Kelly Garvin; Production Specialist: Tori Abraham

All internet sites appearing in back matter were available and accurate when this book was sent to press.

TABLE OF CONTENTS

Words in **bold** are in the glossary.

A POLLINATION INVESTIGATION

Pour in the sugar and flour. Mix in blueberries. Bake and enjoy. Blueberry muffins take just a few steps. But we wouldn't have the ingredients without a big step called **pollination**.

Pollination helps new plants grow. Sugar, flour, and blueberries all come from plants. You have probably seen bees fly from flower to flower. Do you know what they are doing, besides eating? They're pollinating! They are taking pollen from one flower to another. Do you want to get a closer look?

Let's do an investigation to see what pollination looks like.

Grab some paper and markers or crayons. Draw a big flower. Start by drawing a circle. Then draw **petals** and leaves. Color the petals in a bright color. Cut out the flower. Repeat these steps to make another flower.

Now get a bowl of crumbled orange cheese puffs and a bowl of white powdered sugar. These will be the pollen!

Find two round plastic lids. Put a spoonful of orange pollen in one lid. Put white pollen in the other lid. Place one lid on each of your flowers. Now spray your finger with water. Your finger is the bee! Next, put your bee finger in each lid. What happens?

Your finger has both pollen colors stuck to it. Look at the lids. Do they have both pollen colors inside? Just like bees, you **transferred** pollen from one flower to another!

WHY ARE PLANTS POLLINATED?

Now you know what pollination looks like. But why does it happen? Pollination lets plants **reproduce**. This means plants with seeds make more plants and fruit. We would not have beautiful flowers or tasty fruit without pollination.

Plants also release **oxygen** into the air. We need that gas to breathe. People breathe out **carbon dioxide**. This gas is unsafe to breathe in. Plants take in that gas. This makes our air safe to breathe.

Pollinators don't know they are helping plants and people. They are just eating! When bees go from flower to flower, they are looking for food.

Bees eat pollen. They also eat **nectar**. That is the sweet liquid inside flowers. This food gives pollinators energy to reproduce. It feeds their young. Pollinators and plants help each other. They also help us!

HOW ARE PLANTS POLLINATED?

Not all plants need pollinators. Some plants pollinate themselves. Wind and rain blow the pollen. This moves it from the **stamen** to the **pistil**. The stamen is the male part of the flower. It makes pollen. The pistil is the female part. It makes seeds. Those make other flowers.

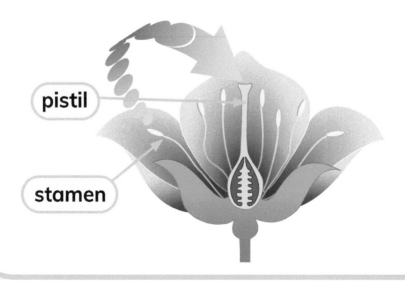

pistil

stamen

tomato blossoms

Peppers, tomatoes, and eggplants pollinate themselves. Most plants still count on pollinators to help.

Remember your paper flower and finger bee? The crumbs and sugar stuck to your wet finger. Pollen sticks to pollinators just like that. Then they carry the pollen with them to another flower.

The pollen falls off into the new flower when the pollinator lands. Pollen then travels to different parts of the flower. Pollination begins!

Let's see where pollen goes first. A bee picks up pollen from one flower's stamen. It carries the pollen to the sticky top of another flower's pistil. That sticky top is called the **stigma**.

The pistil is like a tube the pollen travels down. Pollen falls all the way down. It lands on an egg. That egg grows into a new seed. Seeds drop into the soil. They also can be planted by people. The cycle continues!

Pollination

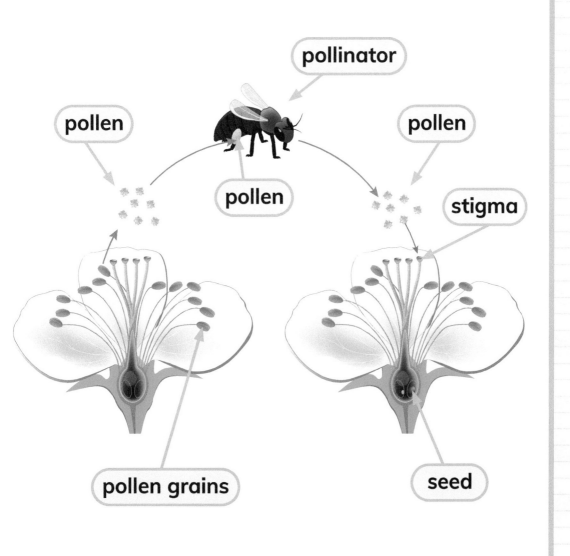

pollinator

pollen

pollen

pollen

stigma

pollen grains

seed

WHICH ANIMALS ARE POLLINATORS?

Bees are the most common pollinator. There are many kinds of bees. Honeybees collect nectar to make honey. Almonds and cherries need honeybees to pollinate them. Other bees pollinate other crops. You can thank fuzzy bumblebees for raspberries, squash, and melons.

Bees aren't the only pollinators. Butterflies and moths are too. So are ants, flies, and beetles.

Some birds and bats pollinate too. Give thanks to both for bananas and other tropical fruits! Bats and birds can fly in place while they collect pollen. Birds use their beaks to reach it. Hummingbirds easily reach nectar from long, tube-shaped flowers too.

Bats use their long tongues to reach deep inside flowers. Bats sleep during the day, so they look for flowers that open at night.

Black-and-white ruffed lemurs are the world's largest pollinators. They open the flowers of the traveler's palm with their fingers. Then they stick their noses inside. They eat the sweet nectar. Pollen gets stuck on their fur. It travels with them to the next flower.

This lemur and palm depend on each other. No other animal that eats nectar is strong enough to open the tough flowers. Sometimes the nectar is the only food available to the lemurs.

Different pollinators eat from different plants. Some flowers have colorful petals and sweet nectar. Those attract more pollinators. Bees like yellow, purple, and orange flowers. They also like flowers with sweet smells. Butterflies like bright colors and sweet smells too.

Some flowers use stinky smells to attract pollinating flies. The corpse flower smells rotten. Flies love it!

Other flowers don't have bright colors or nectar. They don't attract pollinators. Luckily, they pollinate themselves!

HOW CAN WE HELP POLLINATORS?

We need bees and birds. They help plants clean the air and grow our food. But did you know pollinators need our help too? Many bees and birds are becoming **extinct**. People take away their homes. Farmers use chemicals to keep pests off crops. That poisons pollinators.

What can we do? Grow flowers that attract pollinators. Don't spray chemicals. Keep pollinators and their homes safe. Think about bees, ants, and other pollinators the next time you eat an apple or smell a flower!

GLOSSARY

carbon dioxide (KAHR-buhn dy-AHK-syd)—a colorless, odorless gas that people and animals breathe out; plants take in carbon dioxide because they need it to live

extinct (ik-STINGKT)—no longer living; an extinct species is one that has died out, with no more of its kind

nectar (NEK-ter)—a sweet liquid that some animals collect from flowers and eat as food

oxygen (OK-suh-juhn)—a colorless gas that people and animals breathe; humans and animals need oxygen to live

petal (PEH-tuhl)—one of the colored outer parts of a flower

pistil (PIS-tihl)—the female part of the flower that makes seeds when pollinated

pollination (pol-uh-NAY-shun)—the process of carrying pollen from the male part of a flower to the female part

reproduce (ree-pruh-DOOS)—to make offspring

stamen (STAY-muhn)—the male part of the flower that makes pollen

stigma (STIG-mah)—the female part of the flower that is sticky

transfer (TRANS-fuhr)—to move from one place to another

READ MORE

Gray, Judy Silverstein. *How Plants Reproduce.*
New York: Britannica Educational Publishing, in
Association with Rosen Educational Services, 2019.

Kenney, Karen Latchana. *Pollinating Plants.*
Minneapolis: Pogo, 2019.

Raskin, Ben. *Bees, Bugs, and Butterflies: A Family
Guide to Our Garden Heroes and Helpers.* Boulder, CO:
Roost Books, 2018.

INTERNET SITES

Learn About Pollination
sciencewithme.com/learn-about-pollination/

Pollination
brainpop.com/science/cellularlifeandgenetics/
pollination/

Pollination Facts
coolkidfacts.com/pollination-for-kids/

INDEX